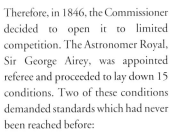

Therefore, in 1846, the Commissioner decided to open it to limited competition. The Astronomer Royal, Sir George Airey, was appointed referee and proceeded to lay down 15 conditions. Two of these conditions demanded standards which had never been reached before:

• the first stroke of each hour had to be accurate to within one second.

• the clock's performance must be telegraphed twice a day to Greenwich Observatory for checking.

III

G.M.GARBUTT

G.M.GARBUTT

Airey's insistence on such high standards led to seven years of controversy, argument and delay. In need of an ally, Airey recruited Edmund Beckett Denison (later Lord Grimthorpe), a barrister and amateur clock designer, as his co-referee. Denison, who was later to take over the project single-handed, was extremely gifted, enormously energetic and almost universally unpopular, but his drive and determination contributed greatly to the eventual completion of Big Ben.

On 25 February 1852 the contract was finally awarded. For the sum of £1,800, E.J. Dent was to construct the clock according to Denison's own design. It was then discovered that the space in the tower would be too small for the clock.

The architect, Charles Barry was blamed, but he replied that Denison should have checked the dimensions before designing the clock which had to be modified at a cost of £100. The clock was finished in 1854 although it could not be installed because the Clock Tower was behind schedule. Thus for five years the clock's movement was kept on test at Dent's factory, allowing many improvements and refinements to be made.

PALACE OF WESTMINSTER

These included Denison's famous "Double Three-Legged Gravity Escapement", which has since become a standard feature in good public clocks. The escapement ensures that outside influences such as wind pressure on the hands of the clock are not transmitted to the pendulum. By this means the time keeping is kept at a constant rate.

The pendulum itself is 4 m (13 feet) long, weighs 300 kg (6 cwt) and beats every two seconds. On the pendulum rod is a small shelf on which there are a number of weights, including some pre-decimal pennies. So fine is the adjustment of this balance that the addition of one penny will cause the clock to gain two-fifths of a second in 24 hours. Twice weekly they are checked by the firm of Thwaites and Reed who took over responsibility for the clock from E.J. Dent & Co. Ltd. in 1971.

The bob of the pendulum weighs 200 kg (4 cwt), the clock mechanism 5 tonnes (5 tons), and the three clock weights total nearly 2.5 tonnes (2¹/₂ tons). Until 1913 it took 30 man-hours a week to wind the clock mechanism, but now it is wound by electric motor. The clock began its life as London's official timekeeper on 31 May 1859.

OPPOSITE LEFT TOP: *Controlled by coins. Pre-decimal pennies are used to regulate the clock's accuracy to the second. Twice a week it is checked – if the clock is gaining time a coin is taken off; if it is losing, a coin is added.*

OPPOSITE LEFT BELOW: *The Pendulum Bob beats every two seconds.*

OPPOSITE RIGHT: *Edmund Beckett Denison (1816-1905); later Baron Grimthorpe. Lawyer and amateur horologist, Denison designed the Great Clock.*

BELOW: *Winding part of the clock mechanism.*

G.M.GARBUTT

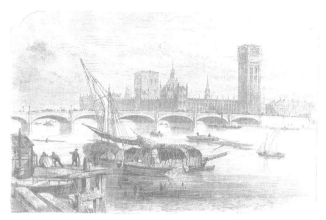

The Clock Tower

As the lower part of the new Clock Tower began to appear it must have seemed to the watching crowds as if it were being built by magic, because there was no external scaffolding. In fact the mighty tower was being constructed from the inside outwards.

Seated on a foundation of poured concrete 3 m (10 ft) thick, the Clock Tower stands 96 m (315 ft) high from its base at river level to its finial at the top, and is about 12 m (40 ft) square.

It is constructed of cast iron girders from the nearby Regents Canal Ironworks; Caen stone for the interior; Yorkshire Anston stone and Cornish granite for the exterior. The iron roofing plates came from a Birmingham foundry. The vast quantities of materials needed were brought mainly by river on lighters and canal barges, and landed on the adjoining wharves. Inside, a climbing scaffold enabled the materials to be lifted up the tower – a 2 kW (2$^1/_2$ hp) steam engine powered a winch which was mounted on iron rails and fixed to timber beams spanning the external walls from east to west. A travelling crane moved slowly around the rails, bringing materials up to the masons and bricklayers who worked from a platform slung below the main beams.

As work progressed the scaffolding was raised, about 1 m (3$^1/_2$ ft) at a time, by six giant screws. In all, it lifted 850 cubic metres (30,000 cu ft) of stone, 2,600 cubic metres (92,000 cu ft) of brickwork, and many tonnes of iron girders and plates. In the west side of the tower, below the clock room, is a vertical air outlet shaft which was included for the ventilation of the main buildings. At one time a large furnace was kept burning at the base of the tower; the used or "vitiated" air from the Palace was funnelled into the Clock Tower, drawn up the shaft by the hot air expelled out at the top. In the south-west corner is a stone staircase which serves all 11 floors. There are 334 steps from the ground floor to the belfry, and a further 59 steps to the lantern.

In the lower part of the tower, a third of the way up, is the room which was intended as a prison cell for offenders from both Houses of Parliament. In the nineteenth century, the Serjeant-at-Arms could be directed by the Speaker of the House of Commons to detain those Members who were rude or noisy during debates. Officially a Member could be detained for what was left of a parliamentary session, which might have amounted to a number of months. In practice, however, no one suffered the shame for more than a day. It was last used in 1880 when the atheist M.P., Charles Bradlaugh, refused to take the oath on the Bible. He was sentenced to one night's custody in the Clock Tower cell, which in fact was a quite comfortable room.

OPPOSITE TOP: *Under construction with no sign of scaffolding. The Clock Tower was actually built from the inside outwards.*

OPPOSITE BELOW: *Charles Bradlaugh in the Clock Tower's prison room. In 1880, Bradlaugh, an MP, was imprisoned overnight for refusing to take the oath of allegiance.*

ABOVE: *The view from Parliament Square one hundred years ago.*

LEFT: *The delicate Gothic tracery of the Clock Tower today.*

VIII   *The "Westminster Chimes" were borrowed from those of Great S. Mary's,
Cambridge, which in turn were based upon Handel's "Messiah".*

The Westminster Chimes

1ST QUARTER

2ND QUARTER

3RD QUARTER

HOUR

All through this hour   *Lord, be my guide*   *And by Thy power*

No foot shall slide

G.M. GARBUTT

X

PALACE OF WESTMINSTER

G.M. GARBUTT

The Clock Face

THE RICHEST DECORATION of the Tower is in the clock storey and above. In designing this part of the building Sir Charles Barry was greatly influenced by Augustus Welby Pugin.

Within the clock storey, projecting beyond the walls of the tower, stand the famous clock faces. They each measure 7 m (23 ft) in diameter and are made of a cast iron framework. Originally they were glazed with a German double flashed opal glass. However, subsequent repairs at various times using English glass produced a peculiar grey and white patchwork effect. So in 1956, during repairs and overhaul, all four faces were reglazed with a Birmingham-made pot opal glass. Each face contains 312 separate pieces of glass.

The minute spaces on the dials are each 30 cm (1 ft) square and the hour figures are 60 cm (2 ft) long. One unusual feature of this clock is that the hour figure of four o'clock is indicated by the Roman IV, rather than the usual IIII. The minute hands are made of copper sheet, hollowed and fashioned to shape. They are 4.2 m (14 ft) long, weigh 100 kg (2 cwt) each, and travel over 160 km (100 miles) a year at their tips. The hour hands are of gun-metal, weigh 300 kg (6 cwt) each and are 2.7 m (9 ft) long.

Behind the clock faces run galleries from where the dials are illuminated. Until 1900, lighting was supplied by a number of gas jets fitted with large Bray burners. After electricity was installed the dials were lit by ordinary tungsten light until 1957 when it was replaced by cold cathode lighting. Today, each face is illuminated by 27 low-energy 55W fluorescent bulbs, each with a life of 60,000 hours.

In the lantern above the belfry is another light – the Ayrton Light, named after Acton Smee Ayrton, a First Commissioner of Works. Since 1885 this light has signalled that Parliament is at work.

It was a dark day for London and the world when, on 1 September 1939, the clock lights were extinguished to conform with war-time black-out regulations. But at the end of the war in Europe, on 30 April 1945, a very different atmosphere was in evidence. At 10.15pm, to the delight of the cheering crowds gathered below in Parliament Square, the Speaker of the House threw a switch and the lights of the clock faces once again shone out over London.

Under each face there is a Latin inscription carved in the stone: "*Domine Salvam fac Reginam nostram Victoriam primam*". The work of Pugin, who used the phrase extensively in his decoration of the new Palace, it is a prayer for the Queen from the Catholic Latin mass and means: "*O Lord, save our Queen Victoria the First*".

RIGHT: *Method of making the bell mould.*

BELOW CENTRE: *The bell was taken to London by ship and pulled across Westminster Bridge by 16 white horses.*

BOTTOM: *A specially made chain, nearly 550 m (1,800 feet) long, was used to hoist the Great Bell in October 1858. Due to its enormous size, the bell had to be turned on its side and winched up in a cradle.*

ILLUSTRATED LONDON NEWS

BIG BEN *The Bell*

ILLUSTRATED LONDON NEWS

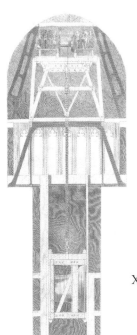

F EW PEOPLE, hearing the thunderous sounds of Big Ben, will imagine the troubled history of that great bell.

It was first cast on 6 August 1856 at Warner's of Norton near Stockton-on-Tees. At 16.25 tonnes (16 tons) it was the biggest ever cast in the country. By rail it went to West Hartlepool, to be shipped to London. It was dropped onto the deck of the schooner, badly damaging the ship, and was then nearly lost at sea in a storm. On arrival at the Port of London it was placed on a specially built carriage and pulled across Westminster Bridge by 16

white horses. Hung on gallows in New Palace Yard it was tested each day throughout 1857.

When it arrived, the bell's official name was Victoria although this was quickly forgotten in favour of "Big Ben". There are two theories of how the bell came by this name: the first suggests that it was taken from the nickname of a champion heavyweight boxer of the time called Ben Caunt; the second and more probable explanation is that it was named after the short, bulky Welshman, Sir Benjamin Hall, who was First

Commissioner of Works from 1855 to 1858 and whose name was inscribed on the bell.

In October 1857, disaster struck during the testing – a 1.2 m (4 ft) long crack appeared in the bell. This produced a flurry of accusations and arguments. Some blamed the composition of the bell metal; others claimed the waist of the bell was too thick. Warner's said it was due to the weight of the bell's clapper which Denison had increased from 355 kg (7 cwt) to 660 kg (13 cwt).

Whatever the cause the bell had to be broken up and recast. This time Warner's asked too high a price, so the job was done by George Mears at the Whitechapel Foundry in London, on 10 April 1858.

In October 1858 the new bell, 2.7 m (9 ft) in diameter, 2.3 m (7¹/₂ ft) in height and 2.5 tonnes (2¹/₂ tons) lighter than the first version, was ready to be installed. But there was another snag – the mouth of the bell was too wide to go up the shaft of the tower. Then someone had an ingenious idea – the bell was turned on its side and winched up in a cradle. It took teams of men 30 hours to raise it to the belfry, where it was suspended from massive iron girders. By this time, the four quarter bells, which had been cast at Warner's Crescent Foundry in London, were in place, ready to accompany Big Ben in the Westminster Chimes.

But even then there were more problems with the bell and the clock. Firstly, the clock would not go – it

was discovered that the cast-iron minute hands were too heavy, so they were replaced by lighter copper ones. Then, when Big Ben eventually started service as a striking clock on 11 July 1859, MPs immediately complained that it was too loud.

Worse was to follow. In September of that year the new bell also cracked. For the next four years Big Ben was silent and the hour had to be struck on the fourth quarter bell.

ILLUSTRATED LONDON NEWS

Finally, in 1863, the Astronomer Royal found a cure: the bell was turned by a quarter turn so that it was struck on a different spot. A small square was cut out to prevent the crack from spreading, and the weight of the hammer was reduced from 330 kg (6 ¹/₂ cwt) to 200 kg (4 cwt). Once again Big Ben rang out, as it does to this day.

By 1859, the total cost of making the clock and bells and putting them in the tower had reached £22,000.

HULTON ARCHIVE

Restoration in 1983-5

The restoration programme used Sir Charles Barry's description in his Illustrations of New Palace of Westminster; Second Series *published in 1865, as reference for the decoration.*

4,000 books of gold leaf were used during the restoration.

39,600 m (130,000 feet) of scaffolding were needed to reach the top of the tower.

ABOVE: *The iron work of the Spire.*

ABOVE LEFT: *The orb and cross are regilded.*

ABOVE RIGHT: *Returned to the original colours – one of the ornamental roses above the belfry.*

TIME TAKES ITS TOLL, even on great timekeepers, and maintenance of the Parliament buildings is vitally important. It was in 1934 when the Clock Tower last received a wash and facelift to repair the damage caused by years of soot, smog and pigeons. The ironwork of the dials was cleaned and painted, and the stonework surrounding them was painted, and gilded.

In 1956 the clock and bell chamber received a much needed overhaul after the buffeting inflicted during the war.

Then, in 1981, the authorities decided it was time for a thorough cleaning and repair of the exterior of the whole Palace. The work on the Clock Tower began in 1983, was completed in 1985, cost approximately 1.7 million pounds, and won the Property Services Agency, who used to look after Government buildings, the 1986 City of Westminster 'Heritage Award'.

To reach the top of the tower took 39,600 m (130,000 feet) of scaffolding, and repairs to the stonework required 3 cubic metres (105 cu ft) of Clipsham Stone from Rutland quarries. Some repairs were also needed to the ironwork. The regilding of decorated surfaces used 4,000 books of gold leaf.

The PSA had problems with the decoration of the carving surrounding the clock faces. On the repainting they sought advice from the Historic Buildings and Monuments Commission, and returned the red, green, blue and gold designs to the stonework. The original colour of the metalwork forming the dial was less clear, so the Commission had to do some detective work. Examples of paint removed from the cast iron indicated that the two most recent schemes were black, but that originally the dials had been a different colour.

The Commissioners advised that two shades of blue should now be used, but the Secretary of State felt that as the black scheme had been known to most people since 1934, and that it is frequently seen by the public on television, then it should remain black.

Nowadays, the Parliamentary Works Services Directorate maintain the Clock Tower.

One of the most famous faces in the world is cleaned.

 XV

BIG BEN IS ALL RIGHT

Down in Westminster last night hundreds of people slackened their steps when they saw Big Ben, or nipped back into the pub for another "mal."

Fact was, the old clock was fooling them. He was determined to be first on this putting back the clock business.

His hands had been stopped at a quarter to eight, and that was the time he showed for a whole hour.

Then they restarted him and he went on to chime eight while all the other city clocks sounded nine.

PARLIAMENT'S 2,062 nights of black-out ended last night. At 9.30 the Speaker, Col. Clifton Brown, M.P., pressed the switch at the side of his chair in the Chamber of the House of Commons and turned on the lantern light at the top of Big Ben's 320ft. tower.

Hundreds of people in Parliament Square and Bridge Street cheered lustily when the light shone out.

"Do you mind taking a look at this watch? I have been all over London trying to get the blessed thing repaired."

Stardom and stoppages

The Man Who STOPPED BIG BEN

And Why

Daily Express Staff Reporter

I LOOKED up to see the time, and hang me if it hadn't stopped. 'Course, they blamed me for putting the ladder up. But how should I know? I'm no clockmaker.

Foreman painter G. F. Weed of Carlingford Rd. West Green, Totenham, talking— the man who ordered the ladder to be leaned against the spindle which turns the hands of Big Ben. Result a man climbed up the ladder and stopped Big Ben yesterday morning.

Mr Weed is in charge of the six men who are decorating and distempering the inside of Big Ben's clock tower. They have been there a fortnight.

It was on Tuesday night that he gave orders' for a ladder to be put against the spindle.

Mr. Weed talking again: 'We came on duty at eight o'clock this morning. The others went aloft. I stayed below.

It must have been getting on for half-past nine when I went out to see the time. It was foggy, so foggy that I had to stare quite a bit before I could see Big Ben. When I did see I saw an eyeful. The clock had stopped.

'Course, I knew something was wrong, but my first thought really was. Well it's foggy, so no one will see.

'I ran up the clock tower as fast as I could—and you ought to have seen me run— and just as I got there Big Ben struck.

'A man had at that moment climbed down the ladder, and the clock was going again.'

Officials of the Architects Officer, the Surveyors Officer, and the Office of Works raced after Mr Weed up the stairs.

They found that not the ladder itself, but the weight of the man on the ladder, had stopped the clock.

At 10 a.m. nearly two hours after he ceased work Big Ben's doctors, E. Dent and Co. had him showing correct Summer Time again.

A POPULAR LONDON CHARACTER since 1859, Big Ben really became an international celebrity with the coming of radio. On New Year's Eve 1923, the great bell was heard for the first time on the BBC, welcoming in the new year. A microphone placed inside a football bladder was installed in the belfry, providing direct transmission to the BBC control room at Savoy Hill. Soon after, it became a regular feature on the airwaves. In 1932 Big Ben went global when the BBC started their Empire Broadcasting short-wave service, which reached millions of people throughout the British Commonwealth. The arrival of television only added to its fame - the clock face made its first television appearance on a New Year's eve programme in 1949 and Big Ben has continued its starring role ever since.

The clock does stop from time to time – twice a year, for example, it is stopped with the start and end of British Summer Time – but it is the accidental stoppage which hits the headlines. Usually these have been caused by workmen leaving maintenance tools inside the clock, but some have been more dramatic; the hands have been brought to a halt by frozen snow, and on another occasion by a flock of starlings. Genuine mechanical defects are extremely rare: in 1944 the pendulum suspension spring broke, and more recently, in August 1976, metal fatigue in the mechanism produced a fault which caused devastating damage in the clock room; bits of the mechanism were embedded in the walls and ceiling and the main frame was fractured. Happily it was only a matter of hours before the clock was repaired and within three weeks Big Ben was once more striking the hours.